WILD EMBRACE

TIM HATCH

BAMBOO
DART
PRESS

LOS ANGELES † NEW YORK † LONDON † MELBOURNE

Wild Embrace by Tim Hatch

ISBN: 978-1-947240-34-6
eISBN: 978-1-947240-35-3
First Printing 2021

Author photo by George Hammons
Cover artwork by Dennis Callaci
Chapbook design and layout by Mark Givens

For information:
Bamboo Dart Press
chapbooks@bamboodartpress.com

Bamboo Dart Press 015

Pelekinesis
www.pelekinesis.com

BAMBOO DART PRESS
www.bamboodartpress.com

SHRIMPER
www.shrimperrecords.com

For Dad

*You're just stumbling through, like
the rest of us. And I hold you
to an impossibly high standard
as a child might*

Huge thanks to the journals in which these poems first appeared, sometimes in slightly altered forms and under different titles:

Apeiron: "Multiverse"
Badlands Literary Journal: "'Pequot's a Fruit'"
Cholla Needles: "Breathe Him Close," "chevron at the intersection of consequence & redemption," "Concerto," "Endless Stories," "Lake Sabrina, 1973," and "Source Code"
Creepy Gnome Magazine: "The Bear"
East Jasmine Review: "Psychedelic Codeine Mobius Strip"
Inlandia: A Literary Journey: "Across the Room," "Bill Speaks," "Boulevard Summer," "Dad Survives His Third Open-Heart Surgery," "Hilltop Sunset (Father's Day, 1985)," "Oedipal Revenge Fantasy," "PCH Sunset (New Year's Day, 2016)," "Six-String Rising," and "the wind loves the lost"
MungBeing: "I Found Your Hair Ties" and "wild embrace"
The Pacific Review: "Christmas Morning," "Expected Miracles," "Helping John Piss," and "Ms. Guthrie"
The Vehicle: "Loathing Las Vegas"

Life is collaboration and community, and in that spirit, I would like to give sincerest thanks to a small army of people without whom, this collection wouldn't exist: Juan Delgado, Omar Moran, Julie Paegle, Chad Sweeney, Jacqueline Wilcoxen, Rosie Alonso, Alex Avila, Lloyd Aquino, John Brantingham, Chance Castro, Michael Thomas Cooper, Michelle Dougherty, Monica Fernandez, Jeffrey Graessley, George Hammons, Nikki Harlin, Allyson Jeffredo, Bolin Jue, Michaelsun Stonesweat Knapp, Orlinda Pacheco, Linda Rhoades, David Stone, Andrew Turner, Victoria Waddle, Eva Warren, and so, so many others. You're all my teachers.

CONTENTS

Lake Sabrina, 1973

Wandering through
a gray day, heavy and wet,

there's little light left, I'm away
from my parents, but I can still see

the sky-blue Dodge van. Far enough
away from my parents that I'm alone

in the forest, alone in the world, away
from the chaos of home: closets

to hide in, my father's countless failed
attempts at sobriety. Trudging

through the woods around the lake, I see
a brightly colored fish (a goldfish? a koi?)

in a tiny creek, little more than a trickle, swimming
where? *Home to the lake? Away from it?*

Could he stay in the creek? Can he do that? Can I?
An adult, thick with brown hair, leaves

and twigs crunching under tan work boots
gathers wood for a fire.

Some words are exchanged: *Won't you get in trouble*
for chopping down trees? "I only take wood

that's already dead." I didn't know wood could die.
I didn't know it could live. The man feels safe.

Responsible. I'm surrounded by trees
too small to hide behind, and I don't know the way

home, so I keep walking and eventually find my way
back to my father, his hands speckled

red with the blood and scales of a trout,
its mouth   opening   and closing. Opening

(his fingers curl around its guts). Closing
(he tears them from its body).

Opening (he calls this cleaning the fish).
Closing (the smell of Coors and Camel cigarettes

heavy in the air, like a low fog,
rolling in off the water).

Bill Speaks

I'm sitting in a chapel, listening to the pastor
who came with the plan speak kind words about a man

he never met. He asks us to bow our heads and follow
through a prayer. The repetition of "Lord" always makes me smile

(not my nicest smile): "Lord, bless this gathering
Lord, as we come together Lord, to celebrate the life of Bill Lord,

and we ask that you look after him Lord,"
and he goes on. If he was saying "Steve" instead of "Lord"

("Bless this gathering Steve, as we come together
Steve, to celebrate the life of Bill Steve"),

everyone would assume he was attempting
a mnemonic he'd read in a self-help book.

My morning was two hours of failing to get students
to participate in class discussion followed by traffic

followed by grading interrupted by an email wanting me
to know I'm not getting an interview

at one of the schools I've applied to followed by traffic followed by
watching one of my best and oldest friends fall

apart over memories of his dad, and now
I'm sitting in a chapel, looking at a black-and-white photograph of Bill

in his high school football jersey, fading into flowers. And here I am,
between my wife and another best and oldest friend, and I'm staring

at Bill, lying in his casket, eyes closed to this world and all its problems,
and I think maybe that's not a bad idea, and I close my eyes,

squeeze my wife's hand, and open them again, looking
for what comes next.

The Bear

He scowls and I know
I've made a mistake. When   he moves
I move
          just   out of reach.

The air is too thin, my mother's screams
do nothing.

I keep a picnic

table
between us. We orbit
two satellites   broken

from their circles. He stops,
and I do too, both
struggling to breathe. He leans

against the table, a coat of forest
green, already peeling, names

carved into it. I can smell
the Coors and Camels. He laughs
and I do too. I will

survive this. He leaps
across the table clawing
for me. His enormous body
blackens the sun.

Helping John Piss

Your gown, little more than an oversized rag
hangs by its fingers. Why do they even
bother with the buttons and ties? I see more
of your naked body than I ever wanted to.

Below the knee, your right leg is a map
of waterways: inlets and estuaries
of varicose veins. Your left foot, ash-
black and dangling, just fails to reach the ground.

You begin to fall backward but my right
arm hooks under yours as my left catches
your back. Your ancient skin, a purple and brown
archipelago of bruises and liver spots, smooth
so different from your calloused handshake.
I bring you upright for these last painful inches.

Your hands fumble under your gown and our eyes
lock in to each other, in silent agreement. Your head
rolls back and I realize your lower jaw hasn't
been jutting out this whole time, you just don't have
any upper teeth. I had no idea.

The echo of water hitting plastic is lost
in your painful roar. A nurse tells you to keep
it down but we tell him to go fuck himself.

A bottle with an inch and a half of brown liquid
appears from under your gown and you place it
next to my iced tea.

I think back to my morning piss, standing
half asleep over the toilet, trying to remember
if there are still eggs in the fridge, wondering
how I'll make the time to come see you.

I take your legs in my right arm, the two of us
forming an awkward Pieta

and I swing them back into the bed.

Expected Miracles

Every child comes into
the world, an expected miracle — squirming
for escape.

Was I the same?

But there's no one to ask, having grown up
in a world of coats and shoes
that weren't mine, that would never fit

me, a thief before I could read
embracing the easily lost
thrill of taking what I wanted but never
what I needed wishing I had someone

to tell me the secrets of being adrift
in the deadwood desert, of the world song
that opens every door, the answer to the yawning

cavernous skies of the north, blue as fury
in the moonlight, clear as a wink
lifting a soft cheek, elusive as the truth

one never quite hears
when God opens his mouth.

Ms. Guthrie

1.

Authority deserves nothing, she'd say. She was
tall as my dad and twice as loud. She wore
big, round eyeglasses that turned her
eyes into novels. When she arched an eye-

brow she didn't need to speak. When she spoke
her words changed the days on calendars.
Her mouth was always twisted off to one
side, an explosion of laughter waiting for

everyone else to catch up with her. She was
fearless, taught us to write our senators, remind them
they work for us. *Authority deserves
nothing*, she told us. Like we were adults.

2.

Her soft blue eyes were locked
onto mine, a smile on her heavily
freckled face. *Once again*

raise your hand if the answer is A.
My arms were crossed. Everyone else
had their hand up. The answer was so

clearly B. She did everything she
could for me, asked if I was sure, pleaded
Seriously? with her eyes, when I said

"You're all wrong." She told
everyone else they were right. She kept
me in class to do multiplication

tables while they all left, laughing
for lunch. She picked up the laminated
times nine card, purple

shape of a seahorse. Her hands were
delicate, a pianist's hands. She held
the eraser end of a pencil, pushed

the point through the 5 hole, the 6 hole
while I gave answers, "Forty five
fifty four." *I'm proud of you.*

That was brave. I looked at her
confused. "Sixty three, seventy
two." She said it took courage to

not raise my hand, with everyone
else. "Eighty one, ninety."
The funniest thing I've ever seen, she

laughed — without cruelty — *but very
brave.* "Ninety nine, one hundred
eight." *That's all twelve.*

3.

    I first discovered Greek Mythology
    in her library. I read how Athenians

    threw bulls in the sea like screaming
    coins into a prayer box. "They worshipped

    Poseidon!" I said. "Like we worship God!"
    No, she said. *Not like we worship*

    God. That was thousands of years ago.
    "Oh." But her words had already failed

    her. *Authority deserves nothing.*
    She said.

4.

    Scott and I, a flushed mess of bruised
    cheeks and torn clothing, a bridge of little-
    boy hatred extending from his eyes
    to mine, solid enough for a platoon of army

    men to stand on, a bridge that kept us
    apart the rest of the year. Ms. Guthrie
    yelled at us, *What are you doing?*
    What's the matter with you? "My dad

    told me never back down from a fight," I cried
    eyes on Scott. "Mine too," he said, staring
    daggers into me.

Then both your fathers are idiots.

That night, my father's fists pounded the dinner table
as he railed about his day and how god-
damn stupid his partners were. Each time
the silverware rattled, I winced and couldn't
remember what Scott did to anger me.

Multiverse

The plug to Annette's curling iron sits
on the tiled bathroom floor, evil
little bastard, waits for the soft
white arch of my foot, sinks
its teeth in deep. I hold back a

scream, kick it out of my way
stumble back into the tub. I
reach out to stop my fall
and, as my palm hits the pink
tile wall, I feel
         the familiar
            shudder of universes
                      being
                       birthed. In one

I step on the plug scream   loud
with purpose, and when Annette asks what's
wrong, I tell her she's a fucking
child who can't pick up her
things. I hobble after her, trailing
blood, as she and the dog back
out of our driveway. In another

      I kick the plug, fall back
into the tub, fracture my spine. She
runs in, sees me, a
broken sculptor's mannequin

and the guilt crushes her. I hold
that guilt   like a cleaver
hack away small pieces
of her, one argument after
another, swinging wildly   to keep her

from the door. Back in this universe, I
grab hold of my temper and wrap
my foot in the gauze I've learned to keep
on hand. I clean the blood, already
yellow on the floor, and I wonder:
In how many universes
born of my childish anger

                              have I squandered her love?

another sleepless night

i surrender a heap in
the surf heaving fetal i
hide from harsh glares
the scorn and sneer of a shovel

sends me back through
walls and time devolved
to early primate i
drag my knuckles on

the bones of the sacrificed
i scream at the terrible sun
who only looks down on

me i grip a femur in
my palm caked with
gray meat and weigh it

against my soul sinking
to my knees the red

clay surf laughs at me
claims me as its own

Christmas Morning

The miracle of Christmas
is that we keep going back
to repeat the ritual
of not rising to my father's
Yuletide bullshit

hung over the holiday
like dollar-store tinsel.

We show up on time and wait
for my brother. As Dad
blathers on about Christmas and how it
doesn't have a goddamn thing to do with Jesus.
Mom dotes on us with coffee, pumpkin bread
and apologies for failing
to finish her makeup.

On the wall, a TV
larger than the kitchen table
frames a dumbstruck Ralphie
as Santa welcomes him to heartbreak
with a shiny boot to the face.

We have thirty seconds of quiet and coffee

before Dad asks Annette if her leopard-print heels belong
to a prostitute. A weary sigh
marks her

retreat to the kitchen, to help Mom
with breakfast. An explosion

of nephews through the front door, tiny
lunatics tackle the anger out of me, spare Dad
from my own explosives.
My brother sits next to him, picks up
sports talk from last Christmas.

In the kitchen, a symphony of spoons
and dishes is lost in the clamor of sharp
controlled breath and unspoken words.

Oedipal Revenge Fantasy

Standing up from the dinner table, my father asks when
I plan on fixing the dent in my truck. *You know*, he says,
when I was your age—

"You know what, dad? When Jesus was your age he'd been
dead for forty years. All of us fail
to measure up to someone."

Yeah, well, at least I wasn't living off my wife.

A flash of blood and I'm outside
myself. The dinner table falls from under me,
chased by the Earth, the solar system, whole
galaxies. Alone, drifting, formless, and so,
so quiet.
I see red dwarfs and nebulous clouds and the colors, dear God,
the colors. The pinks and blues and yellows — the blinding,
piercing white. Slowly it dawns
on me that I'm not in the universe so much as

I am the universe — the same
perfect recipe of hydrogen, oxygen, carbon, and nitrogen
as everything else — and I   am fucking
gorgeous. And huge.

Singing begins, sublime,
glorious, my creation
song, in flawless harmony with myself,
trumpets on a clear, still morning.

All human knowledge, everything
we've ever known, enough data
to destroy a mind,
doesn't add up to a single star in the sky, not even

the memory of a star.

My pride, my ego, my father's
arrogance and disapproval...meaningless.
That I'd allow any one person to define
my life is an act of hubris

so great as to defy sanity.
I cannot hate my father for the simple fact that I am
my father. And he is me and we
are every mosquito flitting
on the surface of every river on every world. And this

sends me home,
and I fall   home   back
to the dinner table   back   in my body
and you know what? He's still a fucking asshole. So
I curl my hand into a fist   a fist   a universe
unto itself, and I sink to my knees
and I punch him in the cock.

Across the Room

A boy gasps and cries
in Spanish
for his mother.

Metal slides on metal
as the key
lime curtain
parts for the doctor.
He gives me lavender

paste and tells me to drink.
My face freezes
in disgust
and then softens as the pain
washes away, like chalk

off a sidewalk. I sink
back, muscles relaxing.
I feel   fragile.   Uncertain

if I'm still here by God's grace
or dumb luck and I wonder

if maybe you felt this way.
Was it the promise
of death or your unreliable body
that left you wide eyed and afraid
to go
to sleep?

Three weeks gone
and I haven't given you a tear.

I curl into a sideways prayer
on the gurney. Across the room
the boy wails for his mother.

the wind loves the lost

there is a boy   lost
in the Santa Anas   wailing
through a lifetime   there are many boys

one is a river
bending through hard country

one is obsidian
beautiful, empty

one is a shore crab
sideways clacking circles in the surf

one is a bloated red sun
ancient and haunted by every mistake

all of them are liars
cringing behind the heavy
curtain of a belly laugh

one is a pleading drunk hands
stuck together
praying in the crawlspace between enlightenment
and wakefulness   where   God
drums distant constellations
sings   to his   children

but the wind is closer than God
and howls without end

Hilltop Sunset (Father's Day, 1985)

Last warmth dies on closed eyes
    tilted toward a shiver. A breeze

sifts through a cluster
    of manzanitas, growing off

the hillside and up, reaching for
    sunlight, like a beggar, whispers

there is no 'deserve' in a language
    older than God. The sky is a battle:

sun rings halo thunderheads
    billowy monuments to the absurdity

of struggle. A pill bug, exhausted
    with conflict, curls away from

the dinner light clawing through
    windows below. Refuses to go home.

Source Code

The *sad* sound of little
brother crying, *so so sad*
as I step on his fingers
a palimpsest of sad as
I walk from fridge to table
calls me to wakefulness, I crush
his tiny fingers *so ugly*
he cries, Dad screams, charges
I'm in so much trouble
so much trouble but I don't

understand, I was just walking
I didn't know there was a baby
on the floor *others*
to watch for I thought
I could walk anywhere *I was*
two years old I didn't know
there'd be someone lying
on the *goddamn* floor *I*
didn't know that was a thing
but Dad jumps, *a rush*
of screams and backhands
what did I do *why*
why is he hitting me *why*
I don't understand *why*
won't he try to understand he
saw what I was doing, he watched
me   *why*   step

on little brother's fingers, *why*
didn't he tell me to stop, and why

why   *why*   *isn't Mom*
helping? I'm two years old

I didn't know anyone would be
on the floor *I will never forget*, I
promise I won't do it again *I will*
never forget, I will always watch out
for others, I will *always*
keep an eye out for Dad
be more careful, I promise.

Home Again

The white sleeves of my shirt
whiter against her darker

skin, still tan from Colombia
the shirt's torso

contours around her curves, hangs

below her knees. She flips her dirty
blonde

hair and smiles. I pull her

back to bed, hold her
close. She wraps my arms around her

like a sweater, we listen
to crows

early on a Sunday morning.

empire's fall

wind hot
on her neck
desperate for another to

run down alleys for
any news from
abandoned social services

through jacaranda flowers
a young mother prays
for citrus groves

a full bottle   a dry bed
for these prehistoric canyons these   crumbling
half-stone habitrails

for a cool breeze
for help
through long nights

I Found Your Hair Ties

Under your pillow
and on the bathroom sink
my bathroom, not yours
God knows why

next to my razor
and in the clothes dryer, the ash tray
in my truck
the vegetable crisper. Half a dozen
under the VCR we haven't used
in over a decade. You'll find them

between the monitor and printer
breeding like insects
under the giant stack of mail
that's been growing since March
of last year. In that kitchen

drawer where we keep long-dead
felt-tip markers and keys
to forgotten locks. They hide

fugitives on top of books
in that eighth inch of space
under the shelf
wedged like secrets
in every fold of the couch.

Concerto

I.

My father's mouth, a broken record
stuck on the same sadistic
song, teeth jaundiced from decades
of coffee and cigarettes, towers

over me, a cankerous storm cloud.
Saliva stretches then shrinks
at the sides, sickly stage curtains
swish open and shut for a
performance that never really begins
or ends.

Deep, sharp pain in my chest pulls
my eyes up to his lunatic glare, right
hand raised, index finger extended.

II.

Like a conductor's baton. He brings it down.

Stupid.
His finger stabs my chest so hard
I wonder if he's drawn blood.

Fucking.
Another stab digs in me
up to the first knuckle.

Loser.
I've never hurt like this.

He keeps laying into me, each downbeat
the perfect demeaning accent
to a dehumanizing verbal spike.
My throat feels tight like
I'm swallowing cotton as he drums
an endless staccato of hate speech.

Worthless. Goddamn. Moron.

His finger comes in wrong and breaks
immediately purpling to twice its size.
Cradling one hand with the other
he comes in close, searches my face,
dares me, begs me, to appreciate the irony
before he leaves, in search of an ice pack.

III.

In the bathroom, I stand
shirtless under the humiliating glare
of the fluorescent, and I count 37
fingertip reminders that I'm stupid
and worthless. I take the blade out
of my father's safety razor and lightly
drag it across my chest, slicing
staff lines for my father's notes.

I stand back and look at myself: Bloody
sheet music for a bastard's concerto.

Loathing Las Vegas

On the casino floor The Damned
sit, collapsed on gaudy vinyl
stools, their skin a sickly, fish

belly white, their faces shine
the color of midnight seawater in
the game-light, almost translucent

at the temples, stained-glass
windows revealing their tweeker-lust for
the ritual of the swiped card and the mindless

mashing of the button, staring
at their god, blinded by his
radiance, stealing glimpses of oblivion

as it plows through their retirement
and their children's inheritance.
Their mutated lizard brains look

back into the mist, vaguely
calling forward a half-memory
of a TV commercial for reverse

mortgages and swipe their cards, one last
sacrifice, one last shot. The casino
coffee shop is nearly empty

at the dinner hour. Three
booths down, sitting across
the table from an old man

who's visibly angry with the keno
display, sits a gorgon. A black
leather poor-boy hat sits

on top of her peroxide kinky
curls, her red clay lips pulled
tightly across her mouth, her skull

intent on bursting through her face
skin the blue white of nonfat
milk. Her right hand teases

the rim of enormous dark shades
her tourmaline eyes faintly glowing
behind them. The keno girl glides

past, a shark, never resting
always hunting, her empty button
eyes indifferently scanning the room.

Out by the pool, the chlorine fumes
hate-fuck their way into
the nostrils of the defeated parents

who wonder what the hell they were thinking
desperately wishing they had a tab
of acid or a bag of shrooms or anything

that might help them appreciate this
Boschian hellscape. It's after
dark now, the sexy people are

long gone, off to have sexy
evenings in sexy clubs, with names like
Misdemeanor and *Cyst*. An enormous

toddler sits at the end of a chaise
lounge, sucking ketchup out
of ketchup packets, his parents oblivious

as they argue over where to take
the screaming children for dinner.
Nowhere is far enough away from here.

Boulevard Summer

3am neon snakes writhe up the hood
    my 77 'chero, windshield lit up like
        a heat-wave Christmas by the vacant

glow of traffic. The road, itself
    a faded star, refuses to age
        with grace, blind to its own, beautiful, beat

up dignity in the blocks surrounding Hollywood
    High, stopping every few blocks
        as it moves west, for more

work to be done, another short term
    procedure, something to be filled, lifted, replaced
        removed. The shooting star of my cherry

tipped cigarette, lands in gutters
    filled with crushed cigarette boxes
        and cracked hypos that can't be unseen

or forgotten   denial is now
    complete as we roll past
        a manic gallery of fashionable

junkies and the tragically hip
    milling about The Roxy, zombies
        in black leather.

kabuki nightmare

oily-black nimbus birds slam
into the clear pool rip smiles from
the spines of giant koi that writhe and thrash in
a silent kabuki speckled sanguine rainbow

of gold fading to black
                              inside the geisha
finishes her sculpture with fierce precision
a blue floral rice bowl is placed on
an ancient teacup forming a porcelain mushroom

delicate fingers spear living anchovies
to clay plates with hatpins carved from feral
hurricanes   secrets   spill from gasping

maws
        chopsticks curl on tails rise
and fall to a dying beat the geisha's mouth
widens and her hands reunite as she turns
circuit-board eyes to the choreographed
frenzy of the dying koi and their winged lovers

Psychedelic Codeine Mobius Strip

i.

Laughing at the news with God

is the only sensible way
to ride out a head cold. I'm wearing

thirty-dollar socks and I'm pretty sure
my feet   have an erection.

My internal organs
are compressed

I have weak thumbs
and a mouthful of disease. Netflix

and Hell are kind of the same thing
kind of perfect on a cold day, but

I want to go outside
run   jump   ride a bike   eat

mystery meat on a stick.

ii.

I stood in front of a 7-Eleven
without my penis

selling a wide variety of pork pie hats
(as you do).

My mother crouched nearby
in the underbrush

blood stringing off her chin
eating a sable.

iii.

Glossy, early-morning
memories of cheating

on women. I wish
I could blame it on being younger.

Where on earth is 6am?

iv.

in my mind   in the mirror
          my beard says
walt whitman   *hey man, got any change?*

v.

The future was supposed to be flying
cars and teleportation   not bagging

our own groceries and televisions
that tweet. #bullshit

vi.

Write to Congress! Demand they solve
all 32,000 FreeCell games!
Demand they recognize orange
as a primary color! Is there any problem
America can't solve?

vii.

Wish I still had my old Pee Chee
folders. The ones with the right
colors (dried blood on goldenrod).

viii.

Is this really   every week?
All this   mayhem? This bombing
of countries with toys? To save   face?

chevron at the intersection of consequence & redemption

dry wind scrapes
    over jigsaw lips

horseshoe-nail christ
    holds key rings

makita girls smile
    secrets through

coffee-ring
    daydreams

deep knuckles
    crust blood

red hands so cold
    they sting

Endless Stories

In my parents' house, I put cartons
of soy milk and egg
whites in the fridge, close
the door. It's an earthy rust
color I'm not sure is
sold anymore. I lean
back against the counter, look around
their kitchen. It's the same brown-on-
tan, mid-70s nightmare
it's always been. Chimes from
my phone tell me I have
an email from the foster
agency. I could carve

a model of this house — eyes
closed — only now I'm seeing
things, like these wall tiles with earthy
two-tone sketches of vegetables next
to recipes my mother never made, these
tiles that faded like days
into years, invisible constants
like monsters in the garage.

The Potato Leek Soup tiles are where
the Father's Day backhand happened. I
remember his thick, metal watch, wide-
eyed rage, and the feel of my pulse
through my cheek, where he got me, but I

do not remember that recipe. I walk into
the family room, the darkest corners
of the house. The remains of a marlin
caught in Mexico, the horns
of a giant steer, a boar's skull, hang
on dark, wood-panel walls. We
stood together here, in 1980,
when he promised he'd stop
drinking. I walk out, past the living

room, where Spode bone china
plates, untouched by food, are housed
in Victorian cherrywood cabinets. I was
reading Daredevil comics on the floral
print couch, Christmas morning, 1988
when he came in and told me *real men
show appreciation for their mothers*
on Christmas. Sometimes

I'm completely lost here, in this
stranger's home I grew up in
a single floor built on endless stories.

In the foyer, ghosts
gather like dust on the red tile
floor, the door to his bedroom just five
feet away. I stop, listen,
wonder what it is I hope to
hear. Snoring. I let him sleep.

I step out onto the porch, stretching
and take the autumn morning into my
lungs. It's perfect. I light up
a cigarette anyway. It doesn't
even taste good anymore but
the ritual rests over me. I
exhale. Ancestral faces in the smoke
roll their eyes at my silent

oath to quit. He grew up here too,
in this brown house with the red brick
porch. His father, the grandfather
I never knew, chased him
all the way up our steep
hill of a street, beating him
with an army belt. He must've landed
on this porch like a plane gliding

on fumes. For a long time, I believed
all my pain began right
here, twenty years before
I was born. But all that pain
isn't even mine, it began
in the house my grandfather grew up in
or the house his grandfather
grew up in, and I wonder how far

back the houses go. How many
more generations of broken men raising
broken men can a family claim? Answers are

elusive but I pray for them
anyway, as I flick my cigarette
into the damp dirt near the garden hose
blue wisps rising,
as if from a censer at the beginning of Mass.

"Pequot's a Fruit"

your father grunts, and somehow, it
no longer matters who John Stone was
all of history is eclipsed by one old man's
bullshit, and your legs start to buckle
and you half sit, half fall on the edge of
the couch, a couch with deep, fat

lines in the fabric, almost corduroy, a beige
that says *Ross Perot* and *Crystal Pepsi*, that
catches you for a moment before
you hit the floor exhausted by the hurricane
of vacuous nonsense that wails through

the house you grew up in, the house with
the perfect memory, that won't leave you
alone, its ethereal fingers curl through
decades of dust and faded light, flick your
earlobe hard, like a fifth-grade

bully, whispers *I'll never forget, you*
can't ever be someone else you will
always be Panzón, and you keel

to the left, your knees come back to your
chest, your cheek reacquaints itself with
the synthetic sharpness of the shag
rug that smells like Reaganomics and dog
hair and five decades of not wiping your

shoes before you walk inside, and you
go fetal, you have to

give the old man credit, he can still
destroy a conversation in a single
sentence, like a super villain whose
arch nemesis is rhetoric, his commitment
to willful aggressive ignorance, joyous

fearsome, a thing to supplicate before
and your arms wrap around your legs
and squeeze, and you continue to shrink
into yourself, you collapse, a dying

star, a soft iris explodes kaleidoscopic, you
collapse in on yourself so hard not even
light can escape, you will take it
all, your house, memory, family, all
identity, a singularity, one

beautiful heartbeat,
stretched   infinite   across
every century forever
into nothingness.   Until

your mother walks in, asks why
you're on the floor and have you
eaten dinner yet.

me in the window

house crumbles secret
shame shakes me
i need this
emptiness i
love to cry
the way babies
cry words climb
all over me words
stuck in battered
angels throats
bright things only
dream i hear you
call me home
there's only us
home
i find us

Sunset at Duke's Malibu

Gulls hover in the sky, a silent explosion of cotton
candy and citrus groves. Behind us, Pepperdine
business grads drone on in their sterile

business jargon of *going forward, let's sunset that
program and explore third-party solutions for blah.*

Outside, a gull winks   dives
into a gradient sea   resurfaces
a conch spiral of   coral   and turtle hatchlings.

Inside, more jargon *for a robust workflow we'll
need to leverage our synergies with*

blahbitty blah.

A pride of albino sea lions
rises from the surf, slow, forgotten

                  gods just now wakened

gathers on the rocks
barks elegies
        toward continents.

in these stacks

revelation wears perfume
    of mold and the dead skin of strangers

jackets every door a celebration
    of paths every key a terrible night-

mare of a vacant toothless smile
    a finger points at 1000 special blends

courageous skin O Jesus did we really
    say O Jesus how could we

Dad Survives His Third Open-Heart Surgery

Don't worry, Dad, you'll be
talking again soon. I've watched you
breathe through tubes so many
times, but I can't stop looking
at you like someone I don't quite
recognize. When did you get

so goddamn old? Your hair stands
wild, sparse, like a balding troll
doll in its seventies. I want to laugh
but there are so many tubes growing
out of you. I try counting them
but I get to your face, wonder who
you are, and lose count. The two
largest spill out of your bed
ending in clear containers, slow

drip collections of blood and piss.
If you'd died under the knife, things
would be so easy. You'd be
the father who could never live
down his mistakes. I'd be the son
who didn't learn how to forgive
in time, and everyone would understand
the burden of my guilt. I could
be steadfast in the face of grief. Live
my life. It would be an easy

easy lie. I used to punch
the brick wall in the alley until
I couldn't hold a pencil. What kind of son hates
his father like that? What kind of man
sits next to his father's hospital bed, sees
a lifetime of Christmas guilt and Father's
Day backhands instead of a sick
old man on life support? Dad, why
can't I hold your hand and tell you
not to worry? That this won't last?

Greg walks in, presses his cheek
to yours, holds his phone like a mirror
says, "Don't worry Dad, you won't
remember this," then leaves, nodding. I envy
his approach to shitty memories.

Somewhere inside me there's a slow
leak. I know there were never enough
years to begin with, and I remember
when I threw away a prayer for you
to suffer like this
every day. I've wasted
so much prayer, the shame smothers
me, like a desperate hug. No one

deserves this. Your new scar, dried
blood and surgical thread, laced
through welts of old scars, looks like
a black worm eating its way

up your chest. I drag my fingertips
across my own stratified scars
each one a permanent reminder
that you and I will always be
you and I, and I hope—

It'll be alright, Dad.
Try and sleep a while.

Six-String Rising

Rouge on pale cheeks, blush
coins that somehow miss
your hollow eyes, face

emaciated, face white
like porcelain, like a doll
so white I want to draw on it, paint

your real face, not this
sunken still-life of starvation
and shame, this taut canvas isn't

you, this   empty   thing
in front of me, an abandoned
Cadillac, left to rust

in a long-forgotten wheat field I
want to see your face
again, see the smile that says

yeah, this is happening as you
play slide guitar with a burning
candle in a room of screaming

women, the smell of possibility
everywhere
I want to watch you raise the dead

again, with a pick and six
strings, make them dance, John
feral things, make them

sing a three-part harmony with God, sing
a rage of life
sing a story into being, sing of life

life, goddammit
I want
to see your face.

PCH Sunset (New Year's Day, 2016)

Sydney pants in the sand before us, all
ran out. Annette's phone mimics a shutter
as she tries to capture the sky. I lean

back on a massive, tan rock, smooth
and pitted with burrows from a thousand
generations of Angelwing clams. Between

competing sounds of ocean and highway, my eyes
tilt up toward the light, closed, and I
listen to the sunset. I used to live a block

north of the 10, and I used to think, at night
that the endless stream of traffic sounded like
a river. Behind us, I hear only traffic.

If a freeway is a river it's a deformed
mechanical atrocity. No fish. No pulse. Get
close to an actual river, you can hear

the life inside, the steady whisper of water
on the shore. The ocean before us sounds
like the wind if the wind had a plan or patience enough

to see it through, and the shoreline pulses softly
with creation song, stories of lost
gods, dreams of plankton. Nameless. Unseen.

Breathe Him Close

For Mark, who shoved his first child into my arms like it was nothing.

Trygve refuses to let
his eyes close,
sits on me,
oblivious.
My left hand
supports his head
and neck
and upper back.
He reaches for something
to hold. I give him
my finger. His fingers
are too small to close
around it, and he yawns
and they stretch, and I
extend my fingers, too
keeping his tips
on mine. He pushes
his four fingers, each one
shorter than my fingerprint,
into my index, and they bend
backward, just a bit,
and like desert
flowers under a storm
of horses
they could bend a little more.
I want to put him

on the floor, run
away. Be rid of him.
His bones are still
soft, will be for months,
his fingers, almost
nothing, I could pluck them
off his hand, like daisies
from dirt. His skull rests
in my open hand, I could
so easily close it.
I want to throw him
back at his father, but I close
my eyes, lift
my head. Breathe
him close.

wild embrace

After Kristin Bock

i want to be an empty
room far from the din of
the articulated world but

it's all so goddamn
beautiful these stars in the wide
open sky tiny shining

eyes this gut laugh that spills
over the moon that turns
the night a playful shade

of pink so vast
i breathe deep try to take it
into my veins but it's too much

and i feel like i'll burst into
wildflowers in an early
april breeze and i succumb

to the glory the ravenous joy
that runs naked through alley-
ways and i have to stand

still   hushed   breathless
let tears collide with my smile
escaped prisoners on an early

morning highway who already
know how the story ends
who can't not hope

who run   run   through
rivers and forests and disappear
in the terrible wild embrace

About the Author

Tim Hatch is a writer and educator living and working in Southern California's Inland Empire. He earned his MFA at Cal State San Bernardino, and his poetry has appeared in *Cholla Needles, Inlandia: A Literary Journey, East Jasmine Review, The Vehicle, MungBeing,* and several other journals across the nation. His eBook series, *My Bariatric Year,* has two volumes currently for sale (with a third volume coming soon) wherever eBooks are sold. As an adjunct professor, he teaches composition at more colleges than you can shake a stick at, and when he's not doing that, he spends his time with an emotionally fragile Queensland Heeler, an arthritic Beagle, and his wife, Annette, who puts up with his nonsense way more than he deserves.

Author photo by George Hammons

BAMBOO
DART
PRESS

112 N. Harvard Ave. #65
Claremont, CA 91711
chapbooks@bamboodartpress.com
www.bamboodartpress.com